What's In It For Me?

The Driving Force Behind Making Decisions & Better Leadership

Sean McDonald

authorHOUSE®

AuthorHouse™
1663 Liberty Drive
Bloomington, IN 47403
www.authorhouse.com
Phone: 1 (800) 839-8640

Published by AuthorHouse 04/05/2016

ISBN: 978-1-5246-0227-7 (sc)
ISBN: 978-1-5246-0226-0 (e)

Print information available on the last page.

Table of Contents

For Dad

Who taught me how to live ehically

Introduction

The decision-making process goes something like this:

It starts with a **spark**- a person wants something. Or, as a leader, you have to make a command decision.

Up next is the **first instinct.** What does your gut tell you? Never underestimate the power of your gut instinct. It can often mean the difference between success or failure.

Then there's **data collection.** This is the information-gathering stage. You'll need to provide information to your brain in order to get to the next step.

The Great Debate. The first instinct was your way of deciding whether or not to enter into the data collection stage. Compared to the Great Debate, a first instinct is mere child's play. Very few decisions are stopped cold in their tracks because of a first instinct. As humans, we are naturally curious and even though our first instinct may be to run away, there's always that little part of us that wants to go a little further or dig a little deeper. But the Great Debate is the critical juncture. It is the crossroads of the decision-making process. And it has several stages that go something like this:

Need vs. Want – The classic scenario that we've all heard so much about.

> **Now or Later** – Let's expand on this one. This could also be considered the "is it the right time" part of the Great Debate. Throughout human history, fortunes have been won and lost at this stage. Some leaders err too much on the side of caution. Then they wonder why nothing gets done.

Why *this* product, service, or action? Are there **alternatives**? This is the height of bargaining phase - when decision-makers look for the same kind of product, service, or action that may be cheaper. Or they look for shortcuts to achieve the desired results. During this phase, the old saying, "you get what you pay for" is lost or simply ignored. DISCLAIMER: It should not be inferred that the most expensive option is the best or the least expensive option is the worst. However, there have been and will continue to be instances where both consumers and businesses realize that there is some truth to "you get what you pay for."

Is this a **priority**? This is a critical phase. Prioritizing needs, goals, and desires leads to better decision-making. If something isn't identified as a priority, then any decision-making with regard to the non-priority item should be put aside to allow the priority items

or projects to assume......well.... priority.

Finally, the decision-maker comes to the final and most important question of them all. This is the question that your brain REQUIRES you to answer before all of the wiring (and whatever else goes on) in your brain will allow you to make a decision to buy, sell, do, invest, create, destroy, build, write, say, sign, contract, hire, fire, ...the list goes on and on.... and on.

For the consumer, it is the most important determinant as to whether he or she will buy anything.

For the business owner, it's what will ultimately lead to a decision regarding whether or not to do business with a vendor.

For the leader, it is the factor that must be taken into account when making command decisions. It helps to determine the potential benefits or drawbacks for both the leader making the decision and for those whom the decision will affect, either directly or indirectly.

For everyone, it is the very *nature and basis* of every single decision that we have ever made or will make in the future. The question that must be answered is simple enough in its wording but stunningly profound in its effect on human events ranging from the mundane and routine to the life-changing and significant.

That question is: **What's In It For Me? Or, WIIFM. for short.** The acronym WIIFM will be used copiously throughout this book so remember what it means!

In the following chapters, we will explore how WIIFIM affects everything that we do. We'll look at how a thorough understanding of WIIFM greatly benefits business owners that are trying to attract more business, service providers that are in the market for new clients, entrepreneurs that boldly go where they've never gone before, leaders that manage employees who are responsible for executing on action plans and reaching goals, and employees that want to further their careers and lives through professional and personal development.

By the end of this book, you'll have a better understanding of WIIFM, its psychological underpinnings, and its role in attracting consumers to your product. You'll be a better leader. You'll be able to apply WIIFM to yourself and others when it comes time to make strategic decisions. You'll be more equipped to understand how you and other people come to the decisions that are ultimately made – decisions which alter the course of the present and the future, for better or for worse.

The title of this book may lead some to believe that it's about selfishness. It is not. This is a book about VALUE. Expecting VALUE. Identifying VALUE. Finding VALUE. Proving VALUE. Providing VALUE.

At the end of each chapter, there will be summary points as well as some questions for you to answer. Use these questions and their answers to build a plan of ACTion.

Let's begin.

Part I

Decisions

Chapter 1

"Nanoseconds"

The Pitch

The human brain is ridiculously complicated. So let's skip the section on its anatomy. This book is about decisions – how they are made and how you can help others make decisions that will mutually benefit you and them. The business marketplace is fiercely competitive. A person's career, on average, will take them through at least 3 different industries and 10 different places of employment. Then there are those who will decide that they want to start their own business. In any of these scenarios, you will ultimately be involved in selling something.

BEFORE WE PROCEED….. Let's get past the nonsense surrounding the concept of "selling." Selling is not evil. It is not tricky. All salespeople aren't sleazy. Are there bad apples in the bunch? Of course! But when we discuss "selling," it doesn't have to be related to used cars, worthless parcels of land, or volcano insurance. In order to survive, all companies in all industries must focus on the maintenance of new business development by reaching out to consumers that have a need for the specific solutions provided by said companies, answering the WIIFM question to the consumer's satisfaction which, in turn leads to a sale of some kind.

Now before you get mad and start saying (or thinking) things like, "not everyone is in sales," or "I've never been a salesperson," just go back and re-read that last paragraph that talks about the main objective of any company or entity that wants to survive long-term.

Still think you've never been in sales? Imagine yourself as a receptionist at a doctor's office. This is certainly not a career that is usually associated with selling anything, right?

Wrong. While it's true that you're not selling a *product* per se, as a receptionist you ARE responsible for keeping the doctor's patients happy while they wait (to the best of your ability.) You are most likely responsible for answering the phone and making appointments. You are responsible for talking with new patients. What if you're mean? What if you are distracted and the caller perceives that you have something better to do? What if you show no compassion or understanding for patients who have been waiting a long time – because you *know* that's going to happen, right? Guess what happens next – the doctor starts losing existing patients, doesn't pick up new ones, and his or her paycheck starts to dwindle because fewer patients are using his or her practice for their medical needs. Do you *still* think you're not selling? You are selling – you just may not have ever realized it before. What a receptionist at a doctor's office "sells" is **comfort and helpfulness.** You're the point of first contact at that medical practice. You're the one that everybody sees first. If you suck at "selling" comfort and helpfulness, you'll get fired.

That's just one example. But hopefully it satisfactorily demonstrates that you do not necessarily have to be responsible for selling an actual, physical ***thing*** to ever consider yourself "in sales." There are those that disagree with this assessment – saying it's not the same thing. While I respect that opinion, I still believe that if you suck at "selling" or whatever you want to call it, you're going to get fired.

Now what does this have to do with decision-making? Well, now that we've come to an understanding that "selling" is more than just pandering *stuff* to make a buck, it's time to discuss how quickly decisions are made – and they are made based on how well you "sell" what you're supposed to.

A nanosecond – suffice to say, it's pretty small. They say that the first impression is the most important. But some would argue that first impressions have to take longer than a fraction of a second, right? I would say so.... but not much longer. Sometimes, the people that you are trying to attract to a new product or service have made their decision to not do business with you – before you even have a chance to start talking! Take for example – you've agreed to a meeting where a service provider is going to "pitch" you on a new service. Keep in mind that you've asked for this meeting so it's not a "hard-sell" in any way. You're excited to learn and are eagerly waiting for the presenter. You're still waiting. A little bit more waiting. You look at your watch and the guy is almost 20 minutes late. Now you start to get pissed. BOOM! Your brain has already made a decision that this gentleman is not reliable. But wait – your brain isn't done making decisions – it has most likely also decided that the company itself is unreliable, isn't run efficiently, and it's going to be tough to get back on your brain's "good size." And all of that happened in nanoseconds – of course the pot was already starting to boil as the minutes passed and your visitor hadn't arrived yet. But once you looked at your watch – the bubbles really started to form. At this point and in your brain, the answer to the WIIFM question is "wasted time" or "lack of punctuality" or something else – but it isn't the answer that your visitor was hoping to give you. Even if he shows up and apologizes profusely for his tardiness and even if there is a *great* excuse for it, your brain is already stewing and though the brain is a wonder, it's still keeping you skeptical.

This is why I constantly advise people to be early – conventional wisdom, right? But you can't prepare for every eventuality, right? Right on both. But no matter why you're late, you're still late and that will always count against you!

The 4 Ps Or Is It 7 Ps?

The 4 Ps – anyone that has ever been involved with marketing or advertising will be able to name the 4 Ps of successful marketing – product, placement, price, and promotion. Have a great product, put it where people will see it, choose a competitive price, and advertise the hell out of it.

There are a few extra Ps that have been introduced to this concept over time – things like people, process, and physical presence. I'm sure if we all think very hard, we can come up with more Ps. But we're not going to do that.

While the Ps were once the gold standards against which to measure the effectiveness of an organization's marketing, the marketplace and landscape have simply become too complicated for what is really a pretty rudimentary system (by today's standards, of course.) The consumer is smarter. They are also savvier. They also, by and large, tend to ignore most of the advertisements that they come across. Blame Tivo or DVR all you want but I believe that the reasons are more intricate. In addition to the consumer becoming smarter and savvier, they have also become less impressed with traditional forms of advertising. With all of the technology that exists, when losing your smartphone becomes more of a crisis than losing your car keys, and with the "here and now…. *right* now" mentality that has gripped our collective consciousness, the fact of the matter is that organizations must find **more relevant, meaningful, and unique** ways to market their services.

They have to find out what the desired outcome is. They need to define and identify the things that absolutely need to happen to achieve that desired outcome. The reality of circumstances needs to be addressed and realized. That reality has to relate to the desired outcome in some way and if it doesn't, the perception may need to be altered. There will be challenges and obstacles – these must be anticipated and mitigated properly and effectively. And ALL of that must lead to a definitive answer to WIIFM.

Let's add to the challenge by going back to our discussion above on nanoseconds. Organizations have to find more relevant, meaningful, and unique ways of answering WIIFM and they need to do it in a split second. They have to do it in a world that is moving way too fast for a consumer marketplace that doesn't have time to go past the taglines. It's daunting. It's scary. It's also reality. And the nanoseconds are ticking away.

SUMMARY POINTS:

- All selling isn't sleazy.
- Most of what we "sell" doesn't actually cost anything
- Today's consumer is more savvy than ever before in history

ACTion Questions:

1. What do you sell that doesn't actually cost anything?
2. What can you do RIGHT NOW to better understand how your brain makes decisions?
3. How can you get past mere taglines?

Chapter 2

"Defining WIIFM Even Further"

If you're already a business owner or if you are thinking about starting your own business, you are probably accustomed to thinking BIG. That's a good start. In order to stop the whining and complaining and in order to take the next step in the growth process, it is imperative that you think BIG. I'm not advocating that you make dumb decisions – not at all. What I'm saying is that if you plan on moving your business or career to the next level of its potential, you have to have BIG thoughts, BIG dreams, and BIG goals.

You've probably noticed that the word "think" appears several times in the previous paragraph. There is a reason for that. Put simply – if you're whining all the time and complaining incessantly, there is no possible way that you can be thinking straight or thinking at all. The human brain can process an awful lot. We have all heard that most of us use between 10% - 20% of our brain's capacity. Studies have shown that certain emotions and actions use up more brain capacity than others. Whining and complaining are two such emotions/actions. So, let's get back to thinking instead of complaining. Let's start thinking about how we can improve our businesses, increase productivity, increase happiness and fulfillment, and most of all for your business – thinking about how we can add more VALUE to the marketplace. After all, that's what your customers are looking for.

Every customer has certain desires, needs, and wants. Some of these include fair pricing, quality products, and OUTSTANDING service. The list can go on for a while. In all of my experiences dealing with customers, I have come to one distinct conclusion. In addition to all of the aforementioned needs, wants, and desires, there is one that is larger than the rest. Yep – it's WIIFM.

But it's not enough to just have *an* answer for that all-important question. You have to have ***the*** answer that customers are looking for and that answer had better be BIG!

It has to be BIG because things are way too competitive out there for it to be small. For small businesses, this is especially true. And your answer can't be a cookie-cutter answer. Here are some examples of these cookie-cutters that simply won't work:

1. "We offer the best products in the industry." – Really? So the other products are all crap, huh?

2. "We're available 24-7." – Interesting. But you better be able to live up to that commitment.

3. "We are personally involved with our customers – from the top down." When was the last time you were successful in getting directly in touch with the CEO of a company?

Yep, some answers just don't work!! These are just a few. So now you're probably asking how to come up with a unique

WIIFM answer that will get the message across, right? Did you catch that word – *unique*? I emphasize that because your WIIFM answer has to be exactly that – unique – one of a kind- unable to be duplicated by *anyone, anywhere, at anytime*. Sounds like a tall order, right? You bet it is! But this tall order can be filled and it absolutely must be filled if you are going to succeed. And guess what – coming up with a tall order WIIFM answer that works will lead to less complaining and more growing by consumers and employees alike. If the consumer can see AND believe the value and can do it in such a way that is different from the masses, chances of success rise exponentially.

So how do you do it? First, for goodness sake, don't ***ever*** *i*nclude the names of products or services in this answer. People simply don't care about the names of products. I've worked in the financial services industry for just about my entire career. I am often amazed at some of the TV commercials I see regarding a specific financial institution's products. If any financial institution's executives are reading this book – take heed of what follows: *every* bank has checking accounts, *every* bank has savings accounts, *every* bank has CD's. Are you getting the point? Insurance companies and their representatives struggle with this too. *Every* insurance company has term and whole life policies and *every* insurance company has some kind of annuity product. This kind of WIIFM won't work. Put simply, your company's WIIFM answer has to accomplish 3 things:

1. Has to give the specific VALUE to the customer.
2. Must address the BENEFIT that your product or service will provide to the customer.
3. Must WOW the customer. This means that when you give your WIIFM answer, your customer must either say or think "WOW!"

If your WIIFM answer does all of these things – it is already BIG. It will lead to more business. It will help you cut down on the complaining and nonsense (to be discussed in greater detail a little later in this book.)

Your Personal WIIFM

We'll talk more about defining a business WIIFM and how it must be crystal clear to those with whom you wish to do business. But there is also a *personal* WIIFM that needs to be addressed. If you're an employee of a company looking to advance your career, you must find a way to communicate the WIIFM to your boss. A little later in this book, we'll discuss the ethics of personal WIIFM answers but I wanted to mention that embracing the WIIFM concept applies to everyone. Acknowledging it is of paramount importance if you are to come to a better understanding of how decisions are made both at the personal and professional level. If you want to be a better leader of people, communicating WIIFM becomes critical when attempting to create loyalty and teamwork.

Buckle up – the ride's just getting started!

SUMMARY POINTS

- There are personal and professional WIIFMs. Both will be discussed in this book.
- If you want to achieve BIG things, you absolutely MUST start thinking BIGGER than you are

ACTion Questions:

1. Before now, have you ever thought in terms of WIIFM?
2. List your top 5 goals. Put them away for an hour. Proceed to #3.
3. Look at the goals with fresh eyes. Are they BIG enough?

Chapter 3

"The VALUE Proposition"

"We change people's lives." Talk about a great WIIFM response! Wouldn't we all love it if every person, product, or service had the *actual* ability to change people's lives? Now, some do change lives – for better or worse – but there's no argument that lives are indeed changed. But to "change a life" is such a broad and ubiquitous term. Now that we know that relevant and unique marketing is what's needed, "changing lives" seems a tad too generic. It also sounds hokey. (Yes, I just used the word hokey.)

Consumers are weary of the same old sales pitches, the same gimmicks, and the same over-the-top promises that aren't kept nearly as often as they should be. And their fatigue is certainly justifiable. Indeed, just about every company promises to deliver the "best service." Saying this borders on sociological cliché.

People are tired of being disappointed. And they're calling bluffs – more so now than ever before. Organizations are faced with a litany of new challenges. In the past, if someone received bad service, they'd probably tell a few people. But they would be limited to the times when they were in another's company or perhaps talking on the phone. And after a while, the anger dissipates. The situation is put aside.

Fast forward to now…. with the dawn of social media, an unsatisfied customer can express his displeasure to hundreds or thousands of people in seconds. Twitter limits messages to 140 characters. But saying "XYZ Company SUCKS" is way fewer than 140. Facebook has 1.2 billion users. That's about 1/6 of the world's population. We have a 24 hour news cycle where nothing is kept secret for long. Google +, Pinterest, Instagram….. you can get a headache trying to keep them all straight. And let's not forget about Yelp…. seems everyone has an opinion and they're not afraid to share them, good or bad.

You've probably heard phrases like, "rise above the pack," "stand out from the crowd," and "differentiating factor." You know that you have to identify your "WOW aspect." It has to be different, unique, and dynamic. For this reason alone, it should now be clear why saying "we have the best service" is not an option. Everyone says it. It's stale. And once again, people are tired of hearing it and getting disappointed when that promise turns out to be empty.

For our purposes, we are going to use the term **VALUE Proposition** instead of "differentiating factor" or "WOW aspect."

The **VALUE Proposition** is defined as **the reason anyone should listen to you, do business with you, and trust you.** In the simplest of terms, it's the ultimate answer to WIIFM – what's in it for me?

Easy enough, right? If it were only so. Creating a true VALUE Proposition is painstakingly difficult. It requires focus and determination. It requires commitment and compromise. It takes time. But you shouldn't even attempt to sell anything, make a decision, issue an order, or try to lead people until you have it.

There are way too many organizations that overcomplicate this process. They'll create "focus groups" that will meet monthly for a year or more to get it "just right." They'll ask for input from everyone with a pulse. They'll try to sound smarter than is necessary and want to incorporate superfluous or lofty language into their masterpiece. None of this is needed. In order for your VALUE Proposition to resonate, it needs to be simple and short.

Here's the **process** to follow when creating your VALUE Proposition.

Get your senior leadership team in a room. Make time for this. Do not try to coordinate schedules. Do not try to accommodate everyone. Pick a day, pick a time, and make sure everyone is there. Don't invite everyone who works for you. Invite only the people that are responsible for the highest level of decision-making. That isn't to suggest that other people's input isn't important. But this process has to be compartmentalized for it to work properly.

Make sure no one comes in with an agenda of his or her own. The SOLE purpose of this meeting is to discuss and create a VALUE proposition. Nothing else will be discussed.

Have everyone answer the following questions IN WRITING:

What do we stand for?

Who do we serve? Who HAS to do business with us?

How do we change people's lives?

Why are we different?

What problems do we solve?

What solutions do we offer?

In other words, your VALUE proposition is the answer to **WIIFM**!!

There are a couple of "traps" that you must not fall into when answering the questions above. These were stated earlier in the chapter but they are worth repeating here:

Do not rely on "we have the best service" as your differentiating factor. Why? Because **every** company thinks and says that they have the best service. Consumers are frankly tired of hearing it. They are always promised the "best service" and are continuously disappointed when that promise isn't fulfilled. As a result, consumers have become a more skeptical bunch. Put simply: they just don't believe you anymore.

"Everyone" is not an acceptable answer to the question, "who do we serve?" You must narrow it down. To do that, you have to identify a niche or target market. (More on this in the next chapter.)

Once everyone has answered those questions, it's time to start discussing the responses. <u>This will take time.</u> In all likelihood, you'll need to block out an entire morning or afternoon for this or perhaps even a whole day. This is important. The time you'll have to commit to this project will rank near the top of the most productive you'll ever spend in your career (or tenure with a specific organization.)

If you're not willing to take the time to create your VALUE proposition (whether you're self-employed or a leader in someone else's organization.) close this book now. The rest of it will not make any sense.

In order to become a better decision-maker, a more effective leader, or change lives, you have to be crystal clear on your WIIFM answer. I've worked with numerous business owners and leaders on crafting their personal or professional WIIFM answers. Most have wanted to start with creating financial projections or a list of tasks. This just doesn't work. It's out of order. When they realize and understand that the *only* acceptable starting point is to create an impactful VALUE Proposition, then and only then are they prepared for the next steps.

SUMMARY POINTS:

- The VALUE PROPOSITION is the answer to the question – "why should anyone do business with you?"

- Crafting an effective VALUE PROPOSITION takes time. It must be unique. It must be specific.

- You must understand VALUE PROPOSITION before you start setting goals.

ACTion Questions:

1. In 25 words or fewer, define your personal VALUE PROPOSITION.
2. In 25 words or fewer, define your professional VALUE PROPOSITION.
3. How can you narrow your focus and get specific on your target audience?

Chapter 4

"Truth"

The thing about the truth is that sometimes it's hard to hear. There's no way around the truth. As much as we'd like to ignore it, doing so often results in disastrous outcomes.

People who run or manage organizations are not immune to the truth. The problem is too many so-called leaders still operate as if nothing is going on outside of their own four walls. These are the same people who wonder why their companies are not growing.

They try to figure it out on their own and get no answers. They're terrified to let an objective 3rd party take a look at the situation. Heaven forbid, as a result of such an analysis, it may come up that there may be some areas where improvement is desperately needed.

There has to be some discussion about the inevitability of truth and the reality of the marketplace. I'm not talking about a fleeting message heard at conferences or training sessions. I'm talking about serious, honest-to-goodness, no-holds-barred, jaw-dropping, hair-raising discussions at the organizational level.

To be frank, I'm tired of listening to the same nonsense about the way things used to be, people being "uncomfortable" with change, maintaining the status quo because it's easier that way, etc. I'm exhausted with tales of CEOs being afraid to try new things because they're afraid of losing their jobs. I'm sick of hearing about organizations refusing to make smart, relevant, and necessary strategic decisions because "the timing isn't right" or "a fraction of consumers won't respond to it." This is no way to run a business.

If we continue to ignore certain truths, things will only get worse. If we continue to accept only parts of reality instead of the entire reality, the things we can presently control will quickly move into the realm of that which is out of our control.

Here are some hard truths that companies and organizations and the people who manage them need to face:

Organizations must adapt to the new forces at play in the marketplace. It's not the other way around. You must go to the market because the days of business just walking in the door are over. If your business isn't growing the way you'd like, one of the reasons might just be that your beliefs on the best ways to conduct business are no longer appropriate for the current marketplace. If you can't recognize that knowing everyone's name isn't a top priority for today's consumers, you need to rethink your strategy or at least do some research. No one is suggesting that you stop giving outstanding personalized service but you don't work at the bar *Cheers*. The truth is that the target market of consumers (Generation X and Millennials) want you to *solve their problems*. If you happen to know their names, that's a bonus. But it isn't necessary.

The "good old days" are exactly that.... old. If your standards and methods are still anchored in the past, they aren't doing any good and are most likely harming your enterprise. It's good that some things never change; however, there are other things that simply must change. The "good old days" are gone. They're never coming back. Let them go or step aside before it's too late.

Not all organizations are lagging behind! There are some organizations doing tremendous things and making smart strategic decisions! Unfortunately though, the hard truth is there are still entirely too many companies that spend a lot of time talking about the need to innovate and modernize but not nearly enough time taking meaningful action. Or they're ignoring these critical realities altogether and hoping things will go back to the way things were.

So the answer to this chapter's WIIFM question – change is inevitable.

Sometimes the truth makes us uncomfortable. If that discomfort results in taking action to address the reality, that's not such a terrible thing, is it?

SUMMARY POINTS:

- The way things were done in the past may not be appropriate or relevant in today's marketplace. If something has to be let go, let it go.

- Organizations and their leaders must adapt to the new forces at play in the marketplace.

- The best-performing organizations are the ones that are embracing the need for change and making appropriate and timely decisions.

ACTion Questions:

1. What are some things in your personal or professional life that need to be let go?
2. Are you up to speed on current marketplace trends?
3. How can you adapt better?

Chapter 5

"Create *Experiences* Instead of Selling Products"

Disney's *"Magic,"* Southwest Airlines' *"Company Spirit,"* and Zappos' *"WOW Philosophy."* These and other great organizations don't necessarily focus on the *products* they sell. They know that if they are able to provide a memorable and extraordinary *experience*, the products will sell themselves. Sure, they have product development teams. But any products that are developed must enhance the experience that the companies are providing to consumers. If this isn't demonstrated, the products simply aren't rolled out.

Here are 3 ways that your organization can concentrate on providing *experiences:*

Be crystal clear on your value proposition. Yes, we're talking about this…. *again*. Why? Because it's important. Simple as that. Lofty talk won't get you very far. Consumers need to understand the value of a product before they will use that product. A memorable experience can help communicate that value. Put a greater focus on the entire experience of doing business with your organization rather than pushing product. Believe it or not, consumers really care about value and brand. They need specifics. They need clarity. They need reasons. Give them what they need.

Have a thorough understanding of your target market. Think about this – if you are a student in a classroom, you want the teachers/professors to have a thorough understanding of the subject matter, right? You want them to have certain skills, abilities, and credentials. Most of all, you want them to relate to you in some way. Consumers need to believe that the companies with whom they do business understand what they are experiencing, know about their surroundings and circumstances, can relate to their challenges and share their successes. If your organization has not done research studies related to demographics, consumer behavior, household financials, and employment on its service area, target market, or community – it will be more difficult to relate to the consumers in those markets. How can you possibly create a memorable experience without knowing what makes your target market happy?

Position your organization as a "solutions-provider." Consumers with problems are looking for one thing: someone or something to solve their problems by providing a viable solution. Economics 101 tells us that people buy product to fulfill an immediate or perceived need. By their very nature, these needs are fleeting. The consumer may or may not come back to you when another need arises. However, if you are diligent in not only providing product but you also create an atmosphere that exudes your organization's commitment to service, solutions, and experience, the likelihood that consumers will continue to do business with you increases exponentially. There are a lot of people looking for solutions right now. If your brand reflects that your organization can provide those solutions, people will take notice. If all you do is talk about your products, your message will get lost in the shuffle.

SUMMARY POINTS:

- People aren't interested in buying product features.
- The best companies in history have sold experiences.
- Focus on the experience rather than the product.

ACTion Questions:

1. Be honest with yourself. Are you selling products or experiences?
2. How can you turn your best products into the best experiences?
3. What specific solutions do you offer?

Chapter 6

"Get Rid of the Nonsense"

If your company is involved with social media as it should be, you've probably seen the acronym "SMH" attached to posts or tweets. It means, "shaking my head" and is used to express disgust, confusion, disbelief, etc. about a particular situation, story, or circumstance.

In all likelihood, you've had SMH days at your workplace. It's inevitable. People do things that downright baffle or even anger you. It's normal to have days like this. But if you find that you're spending too many of your days in SMH mode, it's most likely because something is seriously wrong and needs to be fixed ASAP.

It is vital that organizations rid themselves of nonsense – in whatever form the nonsense presents itself. Nonsense kills, demotivates, and hurts productivity (and thus, profitability.)

As a consultant, I have the privilege of working with many organizations. Leaders of organizations that seem to be stuck in SMH mode call upon me to provide an objective assessment of what's happening. Believe me, some of these assessments have me not only SMH but PMHO (pulling my hair out.) A lot of the nonsense that I've seen has been allowed to fester for months or even years with countless hours of lost productivity and wasted time.

Here are my thoughts on 5 of the most frequent SMH causes:

Meetings that suck. I don't like meetings. In fact, I hate them. I'd be willing to bet that if you asked your organization's employees what they really thought about meetings, many, if not most, would shake their heads. Never have meetings for the sake of having meetings. If you *must* have a meeting, make sure you have an agenda, purpose, and bona fide reason for taking people away from their work.

Complainers. If you have employees that resist every change, gossip about *anything,* disrupt the harmony of the team, or are just unproductive in general, they need to go! You can't afford to have these people working for you. Here's a policy to implement: "Constructive criticism or even complaints are allowed. However, a potential solution to whatever ails whoever must also be suggested."

Policies and Procedures that are outdated or no longer appropriate. If you haven't updated your policy manual in the last 3 years, you're probably hanging onto things that aren't effective anymore. Perform a hard, candid audit of your policies and procedures (or hire someone to come in to give you an objective assessment.) It's amazing that in today's fast-paced market that's filled with technologically savvy consumers, there are still some organizations that cling to "we've never done it that way before." SMH.

Ineffective Leadership. No one is perfect. But leaders have extraordinary responsibilities. If they're not up to task, it's time to say good-bye. More on leadership later on.

Stifling Creativity and Innovation. Why would you NOT want your best and brightest employees creating and innovating? NEWS FLASH: there is a limit to the number of times a creative employee can hear "no" before walking out the door. Are you going to act on every suggestion? Of course not. But if you're saying "no" because you refuse to take even the slightest risk or are more concerned with your personal reputation than the welfare and progress of the organization, you don't belong in a management role.

Make the decision **NOW** to get rid of all of the nonsense at in your life, at your company, and resolve to stay above the fray.

SUMMARY POINTS:

- Don't be plagued by nonsense. Trim the fat. Get rid of what is getting in your way.
- Get rid of ineffective meetings, products that no longer serve the marketplace, ineffective leaders, and complainers. All of these things are holding you back.
- Don't stifle creativity and innovation. These things should be welcomed at your organization.

ACTion Questions

1. What "nonsense" can you eliminate RIGHT NOW?
2. List your top 3 challenges.
3. Create an ACTion plan to mitigate these challenges.....   RIGHT NOW!

Chapter 7

"Help Them Decide"

Again – we are all in sales in some way, shape, or form. Human beings spend almost every waking minute trying to sell something. Perhaps it is a product. But it could also be an idea or a belief. You may not be selling directly to a customer. You may be trying to sell yourself on doing something. Let's look at a few examples:

You sell yourself on getting out of bed every morning. You go through the steps described earlier in this book – most of them unconsciously. But they happen. Your brain must reconcile the fact that if you stay in bed all day, you're most likely going to get in trouble for not going into work. Or perhaps you are trying to sell yourself on getting up an hour earlier so you can start a morning exercise routine.

Gym memberships are a racket. Don't get me wrong – I'm not knocking exercise. But think about this – go to any gym in January and February and it will be absolutely packed. You'll have to sign up, yes actually sign up to use a treadmill. There will probably be a 60-minute wait. Why is this? They're called New Year's Resolutions. We've all made them. Some people still do. At some point, people make a conscious decision to live healthier. They're going to change their diets, watch less TV, and yes, go to the gym. For all intents and purposes, they're set!

But the hard part is just beginning. Resolving to go to the gym is just the start – and it's the easiest step of the process. I've done it before. I'll be faithful about going to the gym 4-5 times per week. I'll do this for several weeks. Then, I'll decide to skip a day. I mean, what's the harm? It's easy to convince myself that I've earned a break. So I make a conscious decision and come up with a *fabulous* WIIFM answer: **you've worked hard. Your body and mind are well-toned. Take today off.**

If only it ended there. But then the next day comes or maybe it happens a couple of days after that. Before you know it, you're taking more of these earned breaks. Your original WIIFM answer way back when you made the Resolution to live healthier is slowly, stealthily, and surreptitiously being replaced with another WIIFM answer. The first answer is becoming less and less relevant and meaningful. The second, weaker answer is the one to beat.

That's why gym memberships are rackets. Go to a gym in March, April, or May – half of the people you saw in the beginning of the year are never seen or heard from again. Yet, they still have to pay monthly dies and if they were really brave at first, they've already paid for the whole year's membership. Ahhhhh…. Capitalism!

How does this relate to helping people make the decisions that best serve their needs as well as your own? In order to get back to that gym and back in the right frame of mind to stick to the task at hand, that first WIIFM answer has to be recreated, redrafted, and in all likelihood, replaced altogether. The new answer has to be such that it completely and utterly overtakes any notion that your "excuse" WIIFM answer is the right one.

THAT's the hard part!

Fear not, it can be done!

Many people reading this may have gone through some kind of sales training at some point. One of the lessons was no doubt called, "Overcoming Objections" or something similar. Are you nodding? Good. Read on.

Overcoming Objections is garbage. It is filth. Sewerage of the worst smell. It *is* lower than pond scum. And frankly, it's offensive and rude. Your job when making decisions for yourself or when helping others make decisions isn't about overcoming an objection.

LISTEN UP: **It's about crafting a BETTER WIIFM answer than the one that is holding you back. Your weak, wishy-washy, and arbitrary WIIFM answers will simply not do.** That's it! No scripts with clever things to say. No step-by-step process. It's time to get real.

SUMMARY POINTS:

- Overcoming objections is garbage and just makes people mad.

- Your current WIIFM answer might be holding you back. If that's the case, come up with a new one.

- Redraft, recreate, modify your WIIFM answer until it sounds AND feels right.

ACTion Questions:

1. Go back to that VALUE PROPOSITION you created a few chapters ago. Now make it better!
2. Resolve RIGHT NOW to stop "overcoming objections."
3. How can you skillfully and ethically help others decide to do what you think is in their best interest?

Chapter 8

"Story Time"

The best and most successful leaders in history have a lot in common. One of these characteristics is their ability to tell GREAT stories. Think about the bestselling products in the marketplace today. Think about the marketing that goes along with those products. Chances are, there is a storytelling element involved. Telling stories creates *emotion*. And we already know that decisions are made based on emotional response.

Sean McDonald

I speak to audiences around the world and I try my best to start and end each of my presentations with a story. The first one is usually something humorous. It helps people relax and lower their guards – especially those who think that I am only there to try to sell them one of my products or services. Humor is powerful. Many people look forward to Super Bowl Sunday. Of course, people want to watch the game. But people also are excited to see the famous Super Bowl commercials – those $3 million 30-second spots that put smiles on the faces of millions of people throughout the world.

You probably don't have $3 million to spend on a 30-second ad buy. Don't worry. I don't either. That doesn't mean that you can't inject a little humor into your pitch.

The stories I use to close my presentations are meant to stir emotion and passion. As a speaker, I want people to remember my message. Now they may not remember what was on slide 2 of the Power Point but if I tell my stories properly *and at the right time*, they'll remember those. The biggest compliment that I can receive is when someone tells me that my presentation got him or her emotional – perhaps the emotion was happiness, perhaps it was pride of accomplishment, perhaps something else.

When helping people make decisions, your goals **must** include creating an emotional response. Reread that last paragraph – notice the part about telling your stories *at the right time.*

Timing is critical. Properly timed stories can pack the punch that you're looking for. Do you want to really motivate your teams to be more, do more, and achieve more? Share GREAT stories about people who did those things – and share those stories *at the right time!* Start to tell the story when you notice that people might be tuning you out during meetings. Nothing recaptures a person's attention than by loudly saying, "STORY TIME!" Trust me, people will come back into focus. Try it. It works!

Let me give you an example.

One of the topics on which I speak is the importance of social media in business. I could go through statistics and numbers (and I do.) But that's not what keeps people's attention. Many skeptics (as far as social media is concerned) come from the baby boomer and senior generations. Too many companies are spending way too much time (and money) trying to get some of these folks to "get on board" with social media, electronic apps, and glitzy technology. Why? It simply doesn't make sense. My belief is that while it is important to use social media in business, it is also important to understand that not everyone will use it. Therefore, when targeting your audience, focus on the age groups that are *most likely* to take you up on the offer. That means folks in Gen X, Millennial or Gen Y, and of course, Gen Z.

In order to drive this home, I tell a story – it involves my Dad. As I write this, my father is 74 years old – a true baby boomer. He is retired. He worked hard for decades to provide for his family. He is a loyal friend, a veteran, and is wiser than any man I've ever met. But he's not what you would call "technologically adept." And why would he be? He doesn't use things like remote check deposit at his bank. When he was given a beeper from his boss years ago (remember those things?) he scoffed and wanted to give it back. He still uses a flip phone and he is perfectly happy. He knows how to check his e-mail (on AOL) and yes, he does use Facebook. **But getting him to use Facebook wasn't an easy task.**

The story goes a little like this:

We finally got my dad to use Facebook. (Then I go into his background using the information in the paragraphs above.)

Not 24 hours after he was all signed up, he called me from his flip phone and I answered to hear this, "How the hell do I get off Face PLANT?" (Laughter from the audience.)

Yes, he called it Face PLANT!

I said, "Dad, it's called Face BOOK."

He replied, "Whatever! Just get me off of it."

"What happened?" I inquired.

He said, "All of these people want to be my friend." (More laughter from the audience.)

"Dad, that's the whole point of Facebook – to connect with people."

Without missing a beat, he responded, "I didn't like these people in 1978 and I don't like them now!" (Boisterous laughter from the audience.)

So I tried to save the conversation by reminding him that he can always "ignore" friend requests. His response, "well that's just rude." (Laugher from the audience.)

Now, in all likelihood, audience members wouldn't be able to quote any of the facts and figures I shared about the power of social media. But I know for a fact that they remember the story I told about my Dad and his love-hate relationship with Facebook. They remember it because they relate to it. It created a variety of emotions within them. They found themselves laughing along, empathizing, nodding their heads, and agreeing with his reactions and words.

What's the result of telling this story? Much of the feedback I have received highlights that people might still be personally skeptical about this newfangled technology but now have a better understanding that you don't have to target everyone when you attempt to get people to engage with the organization in that manner.

Facts and figures alone would never have achieved this kind of realization. It was the story about my dad that got the job done and helped get my message across.

So to close this chapter, I want you to think about how you can incorporate more stories into your managing, marketing, leading, and WIIFM answers. Remember, the stories need to be as personal as possible and they need to stimulate decision-making emotions and feelings.

What will your story be?

SUMMARY POINTS:

- One of the most effective ways to communicate your WIIFM answer is to tell stories.

- Start with something humorous and then get more serious.

- Personal stories are always best.

ACTion Questions:

1. What are the stories you tell?
2. Are there other stories that might work?
3. Come up with at least 4 stories to help communicate your WIIFM answer.

Part II

Leading via WIIFM

Chapter 9

"Lead with Power and Humility"

"He who serves his fellows, is of all his fellows, greatest." – Dr. E. Urner Goodman

I have a long history with the Boy Scouts of America. I am an Eagle Scout and have held a lot of leadership positions in the organization, both on a local and national level. I worked on summer camp staff for several years. My best friends in the world are those I made through my involvement with Scouting.

The quote above is from the Founder of the Order of the Arrow, a service organization in the Scouts. The purpose and sole duty of "Arrowmen" is to serve others. It's as simple as that. There are a variety of ways to serve, too many to discuss here. Suffice to say that every action, project, or work should be tied back to that very simple goal: to serve others.

People lead organizations from all demographics, age groups, creed, race, and backgrounds. The vast majority of these leaders are good at their jobs. Some could use an ego adjustment. A few fall into the category of "servant-leaders."

The concept of "Servant-Leadership" is catching on. Organizations that use the philosophy often enjoy the best productivity, highest profits, and lowest turnover of employees. As a leader, who wouldn't want those things?

Here are 3 Steps to becoming an effective "servant-leader" and *what's in it for you....*

Share power. It's not all about you. It never was, isn't now, and never will be. Your role as a leader is not to grab power and hoard it over people. If you're looking for more collaboration and higher morale, empower those with whom you work to do more. You'll get to see what they're made of. And they'll get to see what you're made of.

Put the needs of others first. This can be challenging, especially in the world that screams "me, me, me." But it is possible. More than possible, it is necessary. Recently, we are hearing about company owners or leaders making sacrifices for the betterment of their employees. One company executive recently announced that he would pay college tuition for the children of his employees. Talk about a great tactic to achieve employee loyalty! Richard Branson created an unlimited vacation program for his employees. He understands that if employees are well rested, they will be more productive and happier. You'll have to find out which "others first" programs might work for your organization. But start to look for opportunities, right now.

Develop your people. I've always been baffled as to why bad leaders, including those who don't train and develop employees, get upset when their best employees leave. It's not rocket science. Great employees want to increase their knowledge, be prepared to take on additional responsibilities, and be acknowledged for doing awesome things. A servant-leader understands this and takes action. A servant-leader creates opportunities for the best employees. A servant-leader makes it known that he or she values professional development.

If you do these things and really focus on being a leader who serves, you will, by your actions, answer WIIFM. You'll not only answer it for yourself but for those who surround you.

SUMMARY POINTS:

- The concept of "Servant-Leadership" is gaining influence
- Sharing power, putting the needs of others first, and developing your people are the hallmarks of "Servant-Leadership."
- Leaders who serve have a much easier time answering the WIIFM question

ACTion Questions:

1. Which leaders from history embodied the ideal of "Servant-Leadership?" How can you learn from them?
2. List 5 ways that you can be a better "servant-leader."
3. Who are your heroes? Why are they your heroes?

Chapter 10

"Be A Decider"

Leaders are paid to make decisions. There, I said it. If you get nothing else from reading this book, get _**that!**_ Get it clearly. Get it good. Because making decisions is what leaders need to do most. These decisions will include everything from deciding to mentor a promising employee to approving attendance at an educational conference or webinar to separating an underperforming or troublesome employee from the organization.

Sean McDonald

Terrible leaders shirk their responsibilities to make decisions. They pass off the burden. They simply ignore matters. They keep kicking the proverbial can down the road by taking an extraordinary amount of time to "review" everything. If you're still "reviewing" something a month or two *after* you've received it, you're not serious about it. Move on. What do I mean?

I'll give you an example from my own business. Potential clients will contact me to get more information about my programs. They'll often ask me to send them a written proposal containing more details of the services or products that I might suggest based on their specific pain points. First, I don't ever "just send information." That's a waste of my time – most of the information that you need about my company can be found on my website. Second, I'll only take the time to write a proposal *after* I've had a conversation with you to find out more about your goals and current situation. Think about it – how could *I possibly* suggest a solution before I have more detail regarding the problem? I don't mail brochures. I don't even have brochures.

Fast-forward – we've had our discussion and I've written and sent you a proposal. My hope is that I have addressed all of your pain points and provided information on appropriate solutions. I've told you how much this will cost you. Remember, **you asked me to do this!**

Then I find out that you are going to "review it for a few weeks or even months." How lame is that?

Something made you come to my website – or the website of another service provider. You already know that you need solutions to a problem – solutions that you cannot create from within your organization. If you're an astute businessperson, you also understand that nobody is going to help you for free. So you have a budget in mind. If I've done my job correctly, I asked you about your budget during our initial conversation and, if I want the business, I stayed within that budget figure when crafting my proposal.

Here's what you have now: a written proposal that is within your budget and that lists viable and proven solutions to the specific problems you articulated.

If you see what you want, get the "buy-in" from whomever you need and then you should **pull the damn trigger!** Easy enough, right? Of course it isn't. Of course you have to do your due diligence. You might even get proposals from a couple of my competitors to see how they stack up against each other. Chances are that they're all going to suggest similar solutions.

You've done all of that (as you should.) Why then do you need weeks or months to "review" what's right in front of you? The answer is you don't. You're just afraid to make the final decision. So when I call to follow up, you tell me you're "still looking at it" or even worse, you ask me to "call back in 3 months." Ummmm…NO! I don't have time for that, with all due respect. Like you, I am running a business. I make decisions regarding my business every day and the concept of professional courtesy should allow me to expect the same from you.

The point of all of telling you all of this is to hopefully light a spark in you – light the spark that will lead you to the realization that as a leader, you are simply expected to make decisions.

But go beyond that – you're expected (or you should be) to make decisions quickly. When Walt Disney was scouting locations for his theme park in the middle of the Orlando,

Florida swamps and orange groves, he started with a budget in mind and some very specific characteristics for the land he wanted to purchase. When he saw what he wanted, he bought the land. He didn't waste weeks, months, or years deliberating with himself about whether to make the decision. He did his homework, made sure everything was on the level, and pulled the trigger! As a result, Walt Disney World, the largest and most-visited entertainment resort in the world was born.

Find the courage then to be a decider.

After you decide, what's next?

Read on!

SUMMARY POINTS:

- The best leaders in history were all deciders.
- Make decisions quickly and confidently.
- After you've done all of your due diligence, there is nothing left but to make a decision.

ACTion Questions:

1. What decisions have you been putting off?
2. Make a plan to resolve those decisions RIGHT NOW.
3. How can better decision making lead to a better WIIFM?

Chapter 11

"Make A Plan"

A lot of people make New Year's Resolutions. 90% of resolutions are never kept. There's a reason for this. It's a simple reason but in almost all cases, it is *the* single biggest reason that people don't reach their goals.

Going further, most people never get around to answering the WIIFM question for their resolutions. They don't have a written answer. "If I stop smoking, what's in it for me?" or "if I lose weight, what's in it for me?"

Deciding that you *want* to quit smoking or that you *want* to lose weight isn't enough. The universe won't move mountains to help you do these things if your resolve is too weak. And, as we've seen already, if you haven't answered the WIIFM question satisfactorily, you really haven't decided to do anything.

It is in the very act of deciding that you pave the way for the next logical step – the creation of an ACTion plan. This is where you will identify ***specific*** tactics to use to reach whatever goal it is that you have set.

To be an ABSURDLY great leader, you have to follow plans. There are a few things that every ACTion plan must have in order to be effective. **Pay attention**, as these are non-negotiable!

Written – like just about everything else we've already discussed, your plan will not work unless it is written out. Period. Grab a pen and a legal pad and start writing.

Deadline – set a deadline for each tactic. You need to have an "end" date. Give yourself enough time to do it right. But don't set the deadline so far in advance that you forget about it.

Accountability – once you identify a specific action step or tactic, you must also identify a factor by which you will hold yourself accountable for working toward or completing the action.

Flexible – nothing but death is set in stone. Make sure that your ACTion plans are flexible in that if your circumstances change, the plan can be changed accordingly.

Systematic – there has to be an order to things. Your ACTion plans have to be organized in such a way so each tactic encompasses not just the action to be taken but everything else listed above.

And finally....

WIIFM answer – WRITE it out! For each tactic, answer the question – what's in it for me if I complete this task? It can be a simple one or two word answer. It can be a paragraph or a life story. Doesn't matter. Write out an answer for every tactic. Doing so and being reminded of these answers will help motivate you to keep going. These answers will serve as encouragement tools when things begin to slow down (as they surely will – no one is Superman!)

Take a look and use the chart below to start formulating your action plan. Fill in the first tactic and then complete the 3 columns to the right for the tactic. Repeat as many times as you need for each ACTion step you create.

ACTion Step	By When?	Accountability	WIIFM ANSWER

This is a simple system.

For now, let's keep going.

SUMMARY POINTS:

- You won't accomplish anything without an ACTion plan to get there!

- Your plan must be written, specific, follow a system, and must be able to be held accountable to someone.

- A written plan does no good if it's not put into ACTion.

ACTion Questions:

1. Do you have a written plan for reaching your goals?
2. If not, write one out RIGHT NOW.
3. After you've written it out, revise, get more specific, and WRITE IT OUT AGAIN.

Chapter 12

"The 3 MOST IMPORTANT Words in the Productivity Universe"

Best intentions – we all have 'em! In fact, most of you reading this are probably working through a "To Do" list that you created for today. But you know what's going to happen, don't you? *Something* is going to "come up" which will throw your rhythm and routine to the wolves. That seems to happen an awful lot, doesn't it? You're not alone.

We've all had to deal with those things that have to be taken care of "immediately" or "right away." They can't possibly wait, can they? Well, if we take a very close look at those things that are so urgent, we're going to find as Dwight D. Eisenhower said, *"that which is urgent is seldom important while that which is important is seldom urgent."*

Are there things that actually have to be taken care of immediately? Of course there are. Let's not get silly here. The point is there aren't as many of *those* things as you might think.

There are 3 very powerful words that you can start using *right away* (see what I did there?) which will increase your personal and professional productivity ten-fold. Those words are **"Not right now."**

Read those words aloud – right now. Practice saying them to yourself first, then practice saying them to your subordinates, if you have any. If you want to end the vicious cycle of adding to your "To Do" list or simply transferring tasks from one day's list to the next day's, you must get very skilled at using those three words.

Remember that not everything is as urgent as it seems. Don't forget that you can easily delegate some of these tasks to others. Closing your door is perfectly acceptable if you're facing a deadline and working on something important. So many organizations still have crazy policies such as "managers must keep their doors open at all times." That's insane. If you're allowing unfettered interruptions, how can you possible expect to get your personal work done? You can't. And the cycle will continue.

Say them again – those words – those 3 beautiful, magical words – **"Not right now."** Don't say them simply to escape or shirk responsibility. That's crap. But don't be afraid to say them when they need to be said.

The answer to this chapter's WIIFM - **your productivity depends on it.** If you continue to allow yourself to be distracted by that which is not urgent or important, you're done for.

I love this productivity illustration that goes along with Eisenhower's quote about urgency and importance.

	Urgent	Not Urgent
Important	Emergencies Deadlines Some calls 2	Exercise Vacation Planning 1
Not Important	3 Interruptions Distractions Other calls	4 Trivia Busy work Time Wasters

SUMMARY POINTS:

- If you want your productivity to increase, you must get comfortable with saying, "not right now."

- This is not to be used as an excuse to avoid work or decision-making.

- That which is urgent is seldom important while that which is important is seldom urgent.

ACTion Questions:

1. Make a list of the most important tasks you need to complete. Where do they rank on the importance scale?
2. What actions can you take RIGHT NOW to cut out the clutter?
3. How much does your productivity increase once you answer questions 1 and 2 above?

Chapter 13

"Coaching With WIIFM"

Recently, I was sitting at the bar at an Applebee's in Flowood, Mississippi – having dinner by myself (as I often do while traveling for business.) It wasn't very busy at the restaurant – it was me and another business traveler at the bar and there were a few people dining at tables and booths. The restaurant phone started to ring. And it continued to ring. And ring. And ring. I was getting annoyed – one of my biggest pet peeves is an unanswered phone at a place of business. Finally, the caller either hung up or someone answered – I couldn't tell.

As I sat there digging into my Thai Shrimp Salad (fabulous, by the way,) a gentleman who I assumed to be the Manager began to speak softly to the young lady who was tending bar. Since it was so quiet in the place, I heard the entire conversation. It went something like this:

Manager: "Is there any reason that you didn't answer the phone just now?"

Bartender: "My job is to tend bar. Not to answer the phone."

Manager: "Actually, we're a team here and your job is to do whatever is necessary. Plus there are people sitting here at the bar, customers who most likely noticed that the phone was ringing while you were watching the TV. Don't you think that sends a bad signal?"

Bartender: "I have no idea. I'll answer it next time."

Manager: "OK. Remember – teamwork. And you're not the only one to whom I'll be speaking about this."

Bartender: "OK. Sorry."

Manager: "It's cool."

I smiled. I couldn't help it. This Manager saw a "coachable moment" and took advantage of it. Sure, he could have spoken to the Bartender in a more private setting. But I doubt he knew that one of the people sitting at the bar was a customer service trainer and might eavesdrop a bit. Personally, I think he handled the situation marvelously. He didn't raise his voice. He asked for the employee's input. He reminded her about the concept of teamwork and that 'it's not my job' is never an acceptable response. And he was able to get a resolution from the employee that it won't happen again.

Here are 3 ways to effectively coach your employees using the WIIFM philosophy:

Recognize "coachable moments" and address them immediately: It might be necessary sometimes to wait a few minutes, especially if the employee is still dealing with your customer; however, if you have a "coachable moment," try to seize it right away! Don't wait. Address the situation as soon as it is possible after it occurs. If you wait too long, the specific circumstances will get lost to memory. Call the employee aside and review the moment. Ask for feedback and input. Get a resolution. And remember that "coachable moments" don't have to be negative. You can create one for a positive situation as well as a way to encourage employees to keep doing great work.

Look for the good FIRST: Start your coaching sessions with the positives. Find and review the good in what the employees are doing. Then tackle the areas for improvement. Always ask for the employees' input. But make sure they understand that they're being held accountable for their work. End the coaching session with resolutions about future performance.

Encourage your employees to start/keep a Journal: This is a great way to include the employees in keeping written records of important matters. When they make those all-important resolutions at the end of your coaching sessions, make sure those go into the journal. Ask the employees to jot down any questions, concerns, or suggestions they have in the journal. Review the contents of the employee journals during every coaching session.

Seize "coachable moments," follow the *good-improve-resolution SYSTEM* for coaching, and make use of journals. **The answer to this WIIFM question** should be fairly obvious: the employee learns to be held accountable and the leader creates loyal and productive employees. It's a win-win!

SUMMARY POINTS:

- Coaching is one of the most important responsibilities of leaders.

- Take advantage of "coachable moments."

- Remind those in your charge about WIIFM if they perform exceptionally well.

ACTion Questions:

1. Is coaching a priority? If not, why not?
2. Resolve to find at least 3 "coachable moments" per week.
3. Keep a journal of your coaching efforts. Review it at least once per week. What do you notice?

Chapter 14

"How WIIFM Creates Loyalty"

Here's a dose of reality – those who make up most of today's workforce (Gen X and Gen Y) aren't loyal to companies or organizations. The days of people spending 30, 40, or even 50 years at the same workplace or for that matter, in the same career field are OVER.

Indeed, research shows that the average person just entering the workforce will change jobs up to 12 times and will work in 3 different industries during the course of an entire career. Remember when "job-hopping" was taboo and considered detrimental to your chances of landing another job? That's gone too. Recruiters actually expect to see more of that these days.

Why is this happening and what does it have to do with WIIFM?

To answer that question, we have to look more closely at what drives and motivates the current workforce. The short answer is that it is ALL about WIIFM for Gen X and Gen Y. Let's look at some characteristics of each generation.

Gen X

- Born between 1963-1982 (there are other dates used sometimes but generally, these are the most accepted.)
- Statistically hold the highest education levels
- More accepting and adaptable to change
- Don't respect titles
- Follow *people* (as long as they are good leaders and mentors)
- MTV Generation (remember when MTV actually played music videos)

Gen Y

- Born between 1982-2000 (as with Gen X, there are some other dates used but generally, these are the most accepted.)
- Millennial generation
- Technologically savvy
- High WIIFM demands both personally and professionally
- Interested in working for people and organizations that enhance the social good
- Generation "Me"

Both of these generations are highly driven by WIIFM. Gen X-ers don't really care what your title is and they certainly don't respect titles. If you're a great leader and they can see how following you will help them personally, they'll respect and shadow you. Ultimate WIIFM scenario! Gen Y is much the same and some would say even *more* driven by WIIFM.

There is a danger in believing that in or der to create loyalty from these generations, you simply have to give them whatever they want. That's nonsense. It's unrealistic and downright dangerous. It does mean, however, that leaders should change their methodology when developing and cultivating loyalty in these individuals.

Gen X and Gen Y don't react well to being *ordered* to do things. But they are happy to assume responsibility for tasks if it's clear how their actions will benefit the whole organization, i.e., if their work has its "place" in the whole.

Gen X and Gen Y are looking for true leaders. They are seeking inspiration from those who manage them and they want to be motivated. They want approachable leaders who care not just about themselves but also for the well-being and professional development of those in their charge.

Gen X is concerned about retirement. Not that Gen Y isn't but Gen X is more so. Therefore, Gen X is also looking for more stability in the workplace. They don't mind change as long as they see themselves fitting with the change. Changing simply for the sake of changing doesn't appeal to them. There has to be a reason and that reason has to fit with their personal and professional ambitions.

Gen Y can seem as if they are a bit too entitled. This is not entirely their fault! Business schools sometimes encourage students to set unrealistic expectations for the workplace.

Considering how important technology has become and considering the fact that it's the folks in Gen Y that possess the technological skills companies need, it's important for organizations to set more realistic expectations while ensuring that the employees are encouraged to remain at the same time. It is sometimes a very difficult balance!

Before loyalty is achieved, there has to exist an element of trust. So let's discuss that next, shall we?

SUMMARY POINTS:

- Today's employees are loyal to PEOPLE not places.
- Gen X and Gen Y have very different ways of looking at the world than previous generations of employees.
- A strong WIIFM answer is ESSENTIAL to break through with the younger generations.

ACTion Questions:

1. Are you the kind of leader that inspires and motivates?
2. List 3 things you can start doing RIGHT NOW to be an inspiring leader.
3. How can you better define WIIFM for younger employees?

Chapter 15

"TRUST: Earning It, Cultivating It, Keeping It"

Earning It

By far, this is the step in the process that takes the longest. It takes hard work and considerable effort. Trusting others and being trustworthy yourself are so very important to operate a business successfully. After all, if you can't trust the people with whom you work or if people don't trust you, nothing else will ever fall into place, will it? For certain, you won't be able to answer WIIFM.

How is trust earned? Here are 3 ways:

Open dialogue – Being able to have open, honest discussions is paramount. If you're reading this, chances are you're not in the espionage business so there is no need to keep secrets. Strengthen your ability to start meaningful conversations. Talk about things that are relevant to the tasks at hand. Share insights, goals, objectives, worries, and challenges. Become very good at having this kind of discussion.

Get thoroughly interested in other people – without becoming nosey. It is important that you endeavor to understand other points of view. If you want to build trusting relationships with others, you must become interested in what is important to them. What do their jobs entail? How do their responsibilities compliment and interact with your own? Dale Carnegie tells us to get to know other people. His book, *How To Win Friends & Influence People*, has been on the bestseller list for decades. I think he was onto something important. What do you think?

Be grateful- if you have been able to earn someone's trust, embrace an attitude of gratitude. Be thankful that someone thinks highly enough of you to trust your opinions and viewpoints. Operate as if that trust can be shattered in an instant if you don't work hard to cultivate it (more on this in parts 2 & 3 of this series.) Show other people that you are truly thankful for the trust they've put in you. You can do this in many ways but perhaps the best way is to do what you promise so as not to betray the trust that others have placed in you.

Cultivating It

You've earned another person's trust. CONGRATULATIONS! But now it's important to build upon or CULTIVATE that trust so it isn't lost.

How is trust cultivated? Here are 3 ways:

Don't rush into anything – just because someone has granted you their trust doesn't necessarily mean that you're ready to start asking for things. Take it slow. Take it easy. How?

Continue with open dialogue and more detailed Q & A – this is the "getting to know you" phase. Now that you've earned someone's trust, chances are pretty good that they'll be willing to share more details about their goals and desired outcomes with you. Pay attention! You don't want to miss anything. Listen intently and make sure that the other person knows you're listening by using both verbal and nonverbal cues (body language.) Lean in, keep eye contact, and repeat what they've said. Think of this as Listening 101 because that's what it is.

Give more than you take – find opportunities to do something for the other person before you ask for anything from them. If you're cultivating trust with a business owner, ask him or her about their ideal customer and if possible, refer someone you know. Build a network of referral sources. Pay for that first lunch meeting, take them to play golf, bring them to a networking meeting as your guest and introduce them to people with whom they might want to do business. Be a connector. Show good faith and good will. If you're cultivating trust with an employee, pour on the praise for excellent work, encourage them to do more, and once again, demonstrate how their work is positively impacting the entire organization.

Keeping It

Earning trust can take a long time. Cultivating it is an ongoing process. But trust can be lost in an instant. It can take days, weeks, months, years, etc. to earn it back. Many times, it is never earned back.

So how do we KEEP trust? Here are 3 ways:

DELIVER on the promises you make – It's important to do what you say you're going to do when you said you would do it. Simple enough. Then why doesn't everyone trust everyone else? It's because as simple as it is to follow through on promises, too many people fall short. Are there legitimate reasons why a promise cannot be fulfilled? Sure there are. If an obstacle arises, it should be communicated effectively – not as an excuse but as a legitimate challenge to getting the job done. Communication helps to build trust. A lack of it erodes trust.

Deliver on promises you DON'T make Huh? Have you heard the adage, "Under-promise and over-deliver"? This is exactly what we're talking about here. If you really want to keep someone's trust for the long haul, get very good at giving more than is expected. Surprise the hell out of people! Be bold. Be forward-thinking. Be creative.

WIIFM – Answer this question!! Decisions are made based on the specific answers to that question. Human logic and reasoning are in no small part based on WIIFM. Have a GREAT Value Proposition and deliver on that value promise.

Funny how this keeps coming up, isn't it?

SUMMARY POINTS:

- It can take a long time to earn someone's trust or to grant your trust to another

- Once earned, it must be cultivated through specific actions

- Keeping trust is ALL about WIIFM.

ACTion Questions:

1. What are the best ways to earn someone's trust?
2. How can you cultivate that trust once it's earned?
3. Do you faithfully deliver on all of your promises?

Chapter 16

"The Ethics of WIIFM"

As I stated in the introduction, this is not a book about selfishness. It is a book about VALUE: expecting it, identifying it, finding it, proving it and providing it. Let's discuss the ethics behind WIIFM so there is no confusion about this.

Human beings are seriously complicated. We do things that make us feel better, look better, be better. We help others, we volunteer serving food to the poor and homeless, we donate to charities, and we drop a few bucks into the Salvation Army kettles at Christmastime.

One might look at the previous chapters and think, "well, I'm just selfish if everything I do, every decision I make, and every action I take is to benefit me." DON'T FALL INTO THIS TRAP. Listen, humans as a species have been doing what's best for them for many millions of years – it's called, "Survival of the Fittest." Perhaps you've heard of the concept?

Because the WIIFM question has to be adequately answered before your brain will allow you to make a decision does not, in and of itself, make a person selfish. It makes you human. In a world that needs higher ethical standards, I'd say that acting like a human being is a good start.

If you're still not buying any of this and if by chance you're still reading this, look at it another way. Let's say you volunteer at a soup kitchen once a month to serve meals to the poor. The reason you do it could be anything from the act of helping others makes you feel better or more hopeful for the world to you were once in an unfortunate position yourself and this is your way of giving back. No go back and read that last sentence again. The word "you" and its derivatives appear exactly 5 times in a rather short sentence. Yes, you are helping others. But you're doing it to make yourself feel good in addition to rendering service to the other people. You donate to charity out of a sense of obligation to "do something." Sound familiar? Each time you give a donation, no matter the size, a chemical reaction in your brain allows for the release of dopamine – that's the "feel-good" stuff. It happens unconsciously – you cannot control it. But it only happens when your brain is the recipient of something good happening to ITSELF.

There is no need to be ashamed to recognize and acknowledge the possibility that the good deeds you perform provide direct and tangible assistance to others while at the same time make you feel pretty darn good about yourself in the process. THAT'S humanity! And it's a beautiful thing. It is not something to be skittish about. In his book, *How Are We To Live*, author Peter Singer challenges the belief that human beings are simply selfish and perform good deeds only because of the personal benefits that befall the benefactor. Indeed, ethics completely surround us – it's a question of whether or not we allow them to permeate our consciousness.

> Ethics lies behind many of our choices,
> whether personal or political, or bridging
> the division between the two. Sometimes it

comes easily and naturally to us; in other circumstances, it can be very demanding. But ethics intrudes into our conscious lives only occasionally, and often in a confused way. If we are to make properly considered ultimate choices, we must first become more aware of the ethical ramifications of the way we live. Only then is it possible to make ethics a more conscious and coherent part of everyday life.

For all of its simplicity, WIIFM is an incredibly complex concept, isn't it?

SUMMARY POINTS:

- Acting on WIIFM does not automatically make you selfish
- WIIFM is a need that is at the very root of our humanity
- Needing a WIIFM answer is entirely ethical, if used for good

ACTion Questions:

1. Identify 2 or 3 actions that you take regularly that make you feel great about yourself.
2. How can you explain WIIFM to someone who would question its ethics?
3. Do you understand how conscience and WIIFM work together?

RESOURCE:

Singer, Peter. *How Are We To Live?*. New York, NY: Prometheus Books; 1995.

Conclusion

I'll say it a third time – this is not a book about selfishness. It's a book about finding and providing value. I hope that you found the information relevant and useful. I strongly urge you to complete the ACTion question sections at the end of each chapter if you haven't been doing so all along. Go back and review those answers often. Change them when necessary. Come up with new and creative answers to the same questions.

I wanted to write this book about WIIFM because of my strong belief in the power of value. But it's not enough just to have value – whether personal or commercial through products and services. You have to know how to communicate that value in such a way that your value becomes apparent and appealing to others.

Some might question the ethics of WIIFM – don't be one of them! Throughout these chapters, I've attempted to communicate my beliefs about WIIFM and how it guides our decision-making process and our leadership tactics. I implore you to look for other viewpoints, get another point of view, compare and contrast. That's how we learn to do better and be more.

Thanks again for reading!

Acknowledgements

To you, my readers and supporters – for teaching me more than I could ever teach you.

To the fine people at AuthorHouse, thanks for making my second go-around easier than my first!

To Kevin Canessa for 25 years of friendship and encouragement and for his keen editing eye. Love you brother.

To Christian Suri for his time and honest feedback. He's in Medical school and read this book before you did to make sure I wasn't crazy.

To the Research Librarians at the Harris County Public Library in Houston for their assistance in helping me find the obvious and obscure.

To Sir Jack Campion for instilling in me the love of reading and writing and for always challenging me to do better.

To my Mom and Dad for more than could ever be put to words on paper.

Lastly, to my family, my wonderful wife Susan who puts up with me being "in the zone" while I'm writing and to my beautiful children Leah & Logan – Daddy loves you very much.

Sean McDonald

February 22, 2016

Kingwood, Texas